DRUM CHART HITS
30 TRANSCRIPTIONS OF POPULAR SONGS

ISBN 978-1-4950-9469-9

HAL•LEONARD®

7777 W. BLUEMOUND RD. P.O. BOX 13819 MILWAUKEE, WI 53213

Visit Hal Leonard Online at
www.halleonard.com

The Adventures of Rain Dance Maggie

Words and Music by Anthony Kiedis, Flea,
Chad Smith and Josh Klinghoffer

Intro
Moderately ♩ = 106

Verse
Lip - stick junk - ie...

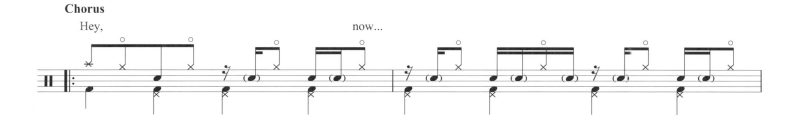

Chorus

Hey,   now...

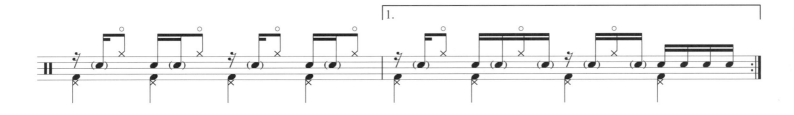

2.

Interlude

Verse

Rain - dance   Mag - gie ad - vanc -

- es to the fi - nal...

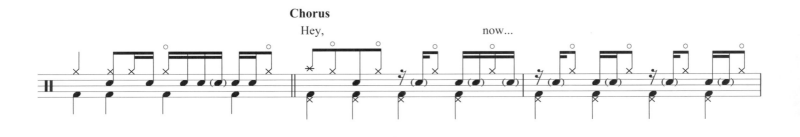

Chorus

Hey,   now...

Guitar Solo

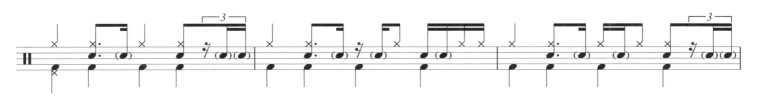

Bridge

You've got the wrong girl...

Chorus

Hey, now...

gradually open

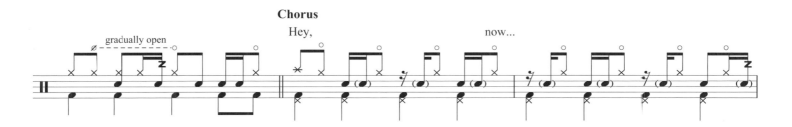

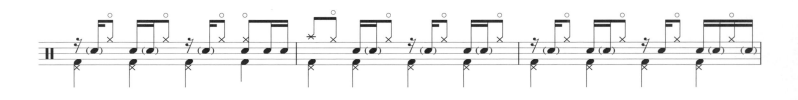

Outro

But not for   long,   girl...

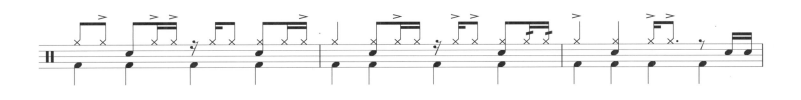

All About That Bass

Words and Music by Kevin Kadish and Meghan Trainor

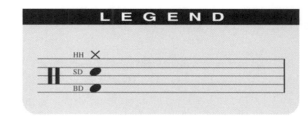

Intro
Moderately fast ♩ = 134

Be - cause you know I'm...

Verse

Play 3 times

Pre-Chorus

Play 7 times

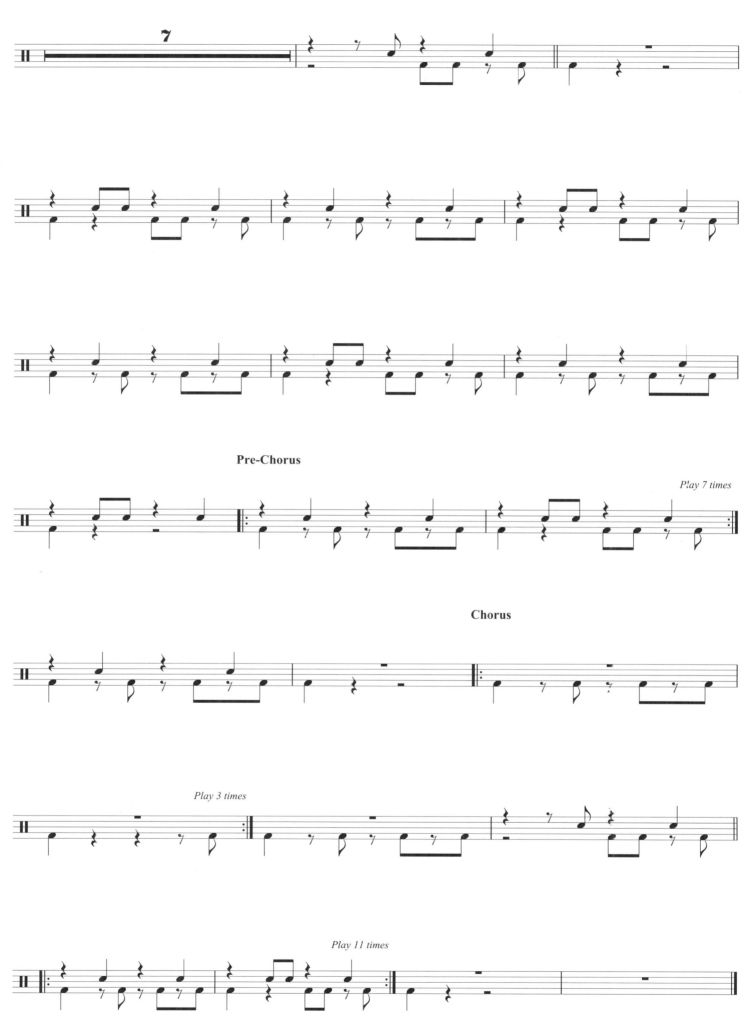

Pre-Chorus

Play 7 times

Chorus

Play 3 times

Play 11 times

Can't Feel My Face

Words and Music by Abel Tesfaye, Max Martin,
Savan Kotecha, Peter Svensson and Ali Payami

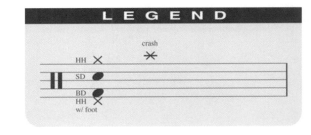

Intro
Moderately ♩ = 108

Verse

Pre-Chorus

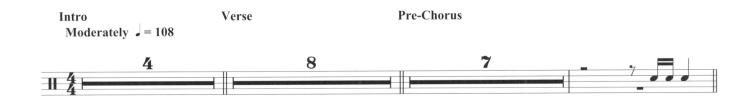

Chorus

I can't feel my face when I'm with you...

Verse

And I know she'll be the death of me...

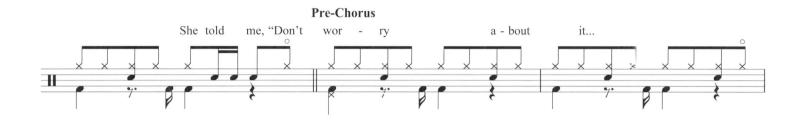

Pre-Chorus

She told me, "Don't wor - ry   a - bout   it..."

2

𝄋 **Chorus**

I   can't   feel   my   face   when   I'm   with

you...

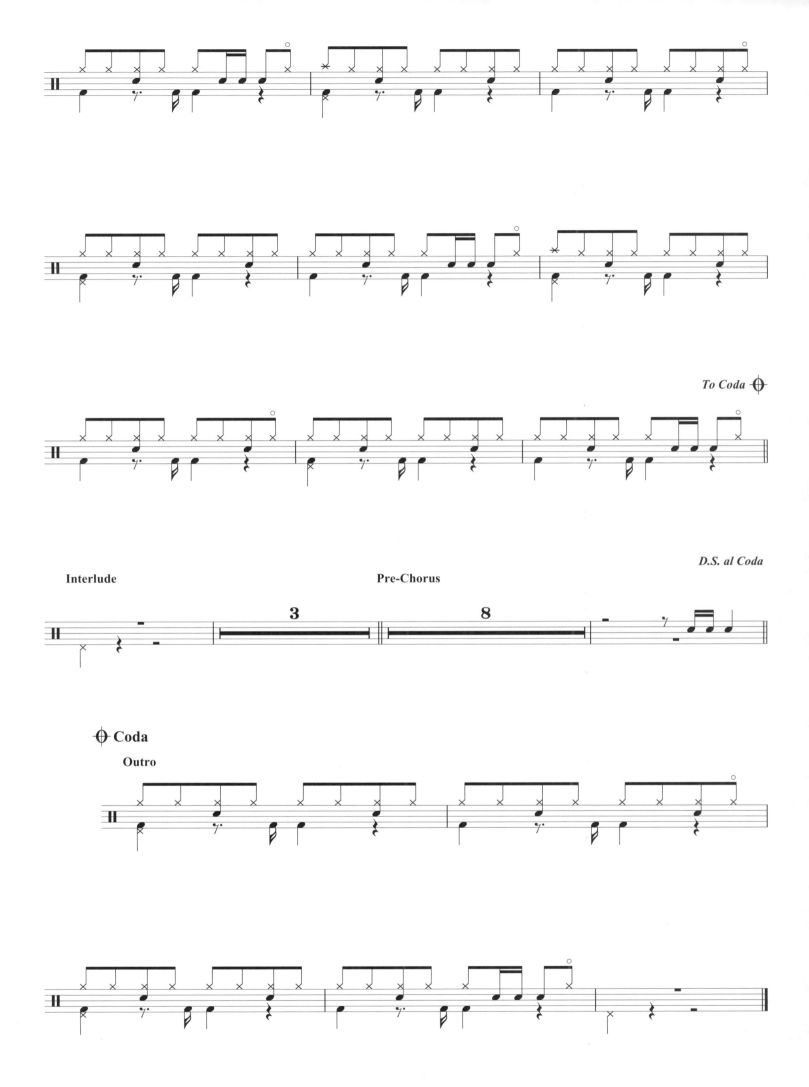

To Coda ⊕

D.S. al Coda

Interlude

Pre-Chorus

3

8

⊕ Coda

Outro

Can't Stop the Feeling

from TROLLS

Words and Music by Justin Timberlake, Max Martin and Shellback

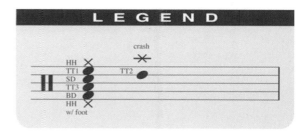

Verse

Oo,   it's some-thing mag - i - - cal...

Play 3 times

Pre-Chorus

Play 4 times   *Play 4 times*

Chorus

1., 3.   2.

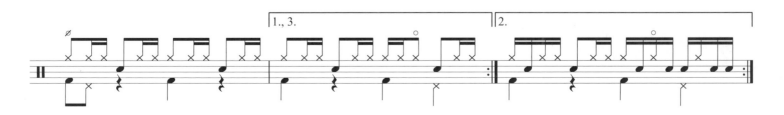

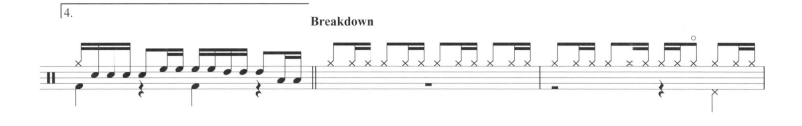

Breakdown

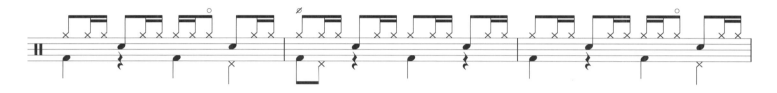

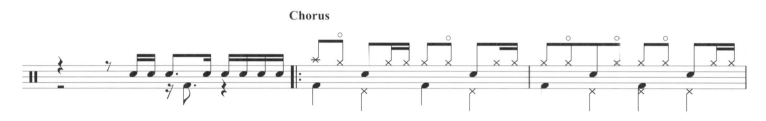

Chorus

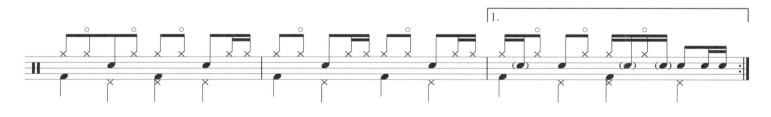

Outro

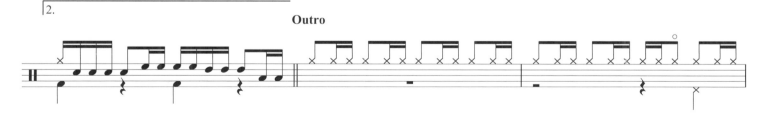

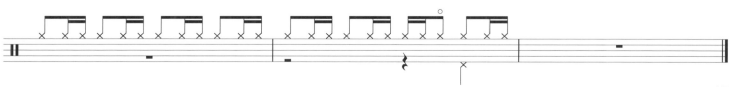

Centuries

Words and Music by Peter Wentz, Patrick Stump,
Joseph Trohman, Andrew Hurley, Jonathan Rotem,
Suzanne Vega, Justin Tranter, Michael Fonseca and Raja Kumari

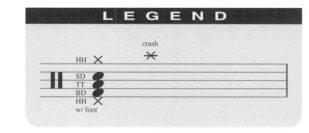

Intro
Moderate Rock ♩ = 88

Chorus

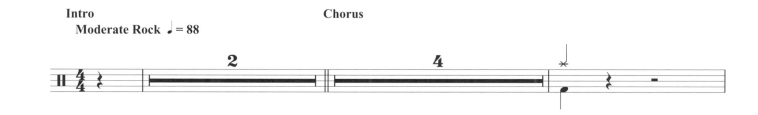

Ma-ma fight my teen-age dreams...

Verse

% Interlude

Chorus

Play 3 times

To Coda ⊕

Verse

I   can't   stop till the whole world...

D.S. al Coda
(take repeat)

Bridge

Happy

from DESPICABLE ME 2
Words and Music by Pharrell Williams

Do I Wanna Know?

Words by Alex Turner
Music by Arctic Monkeys

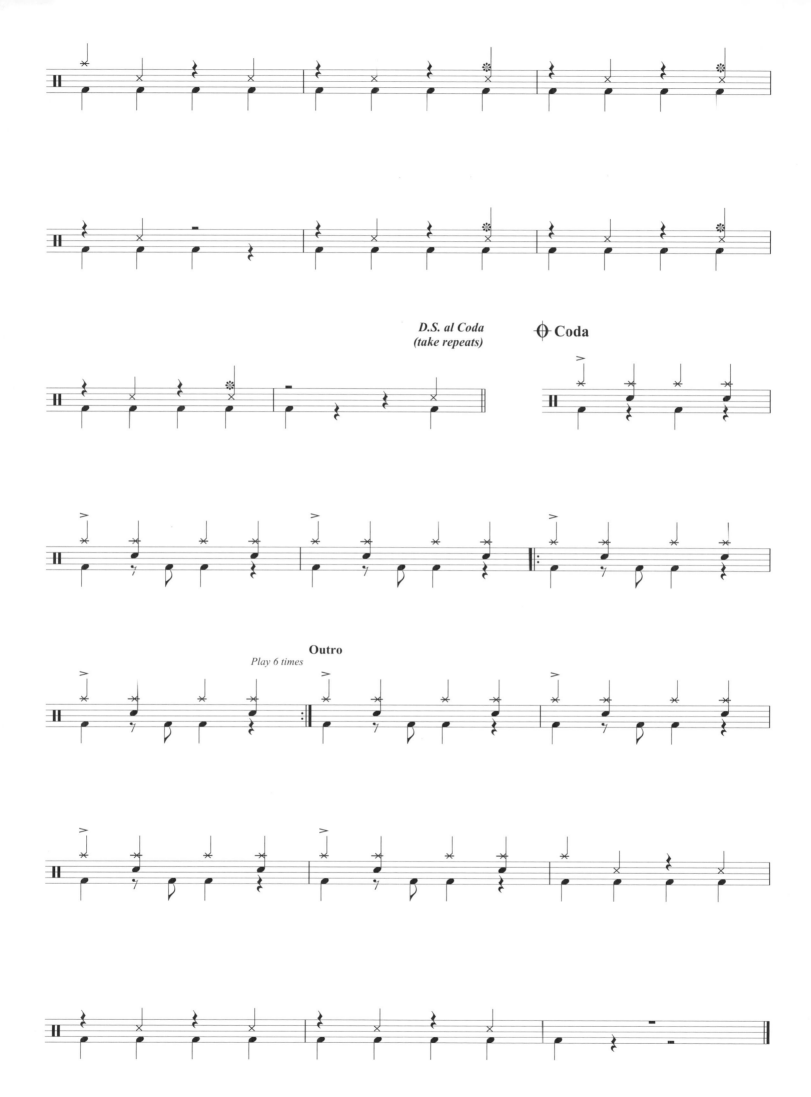

D.S. al Coda
(take repeats)

⊕ **Coda**

Outro
Play 6 times

Ex's & Oh's

Words and Music by Tanner Schneider and Dave Bassett

Intro
Moderately fast ♩ = 140

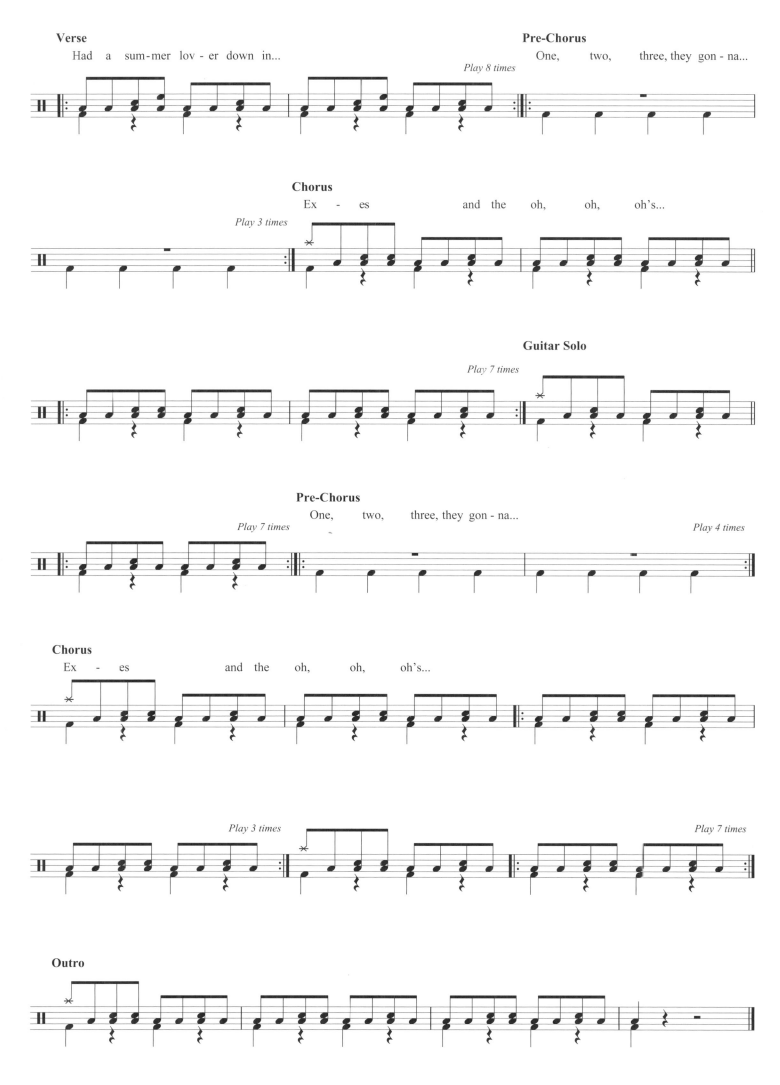

Forget You

Words and Music by Bruno Mars, Ari Levine,
Philip Lawrence, Thomas Callaway and Brody Brown

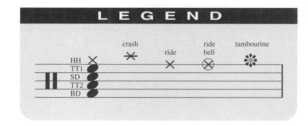

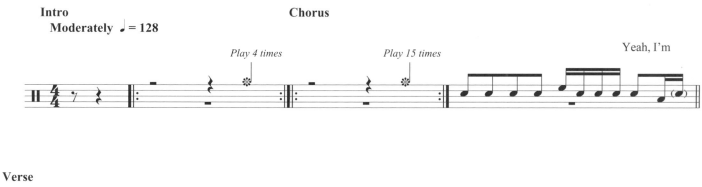

𝄋 Chorus

See you driv - ing 'round town...

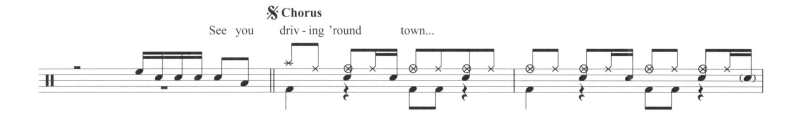

To Coda ⊕

Bridge

Play 6 times

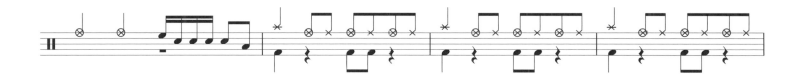

D.S. al Coda   ⊕ **Coda**

Get Lucky

Words and Music by Thomas Bangalter,
Guy Manuel Homem Christo, Nile Rodgers and Pharrell Williams

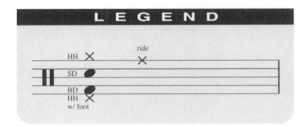

Intro
Moderately ♩ = 116

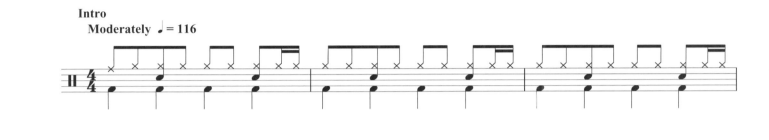

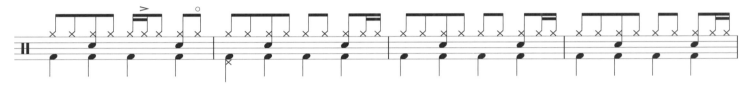

𝄋 **Verse**

Like the leg-end of the phoe - nix...

Pre-Chorus

We've   come too far...

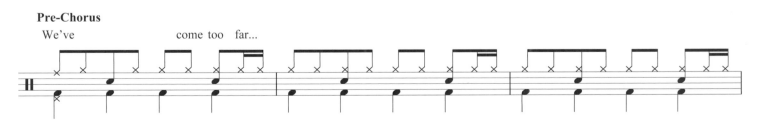

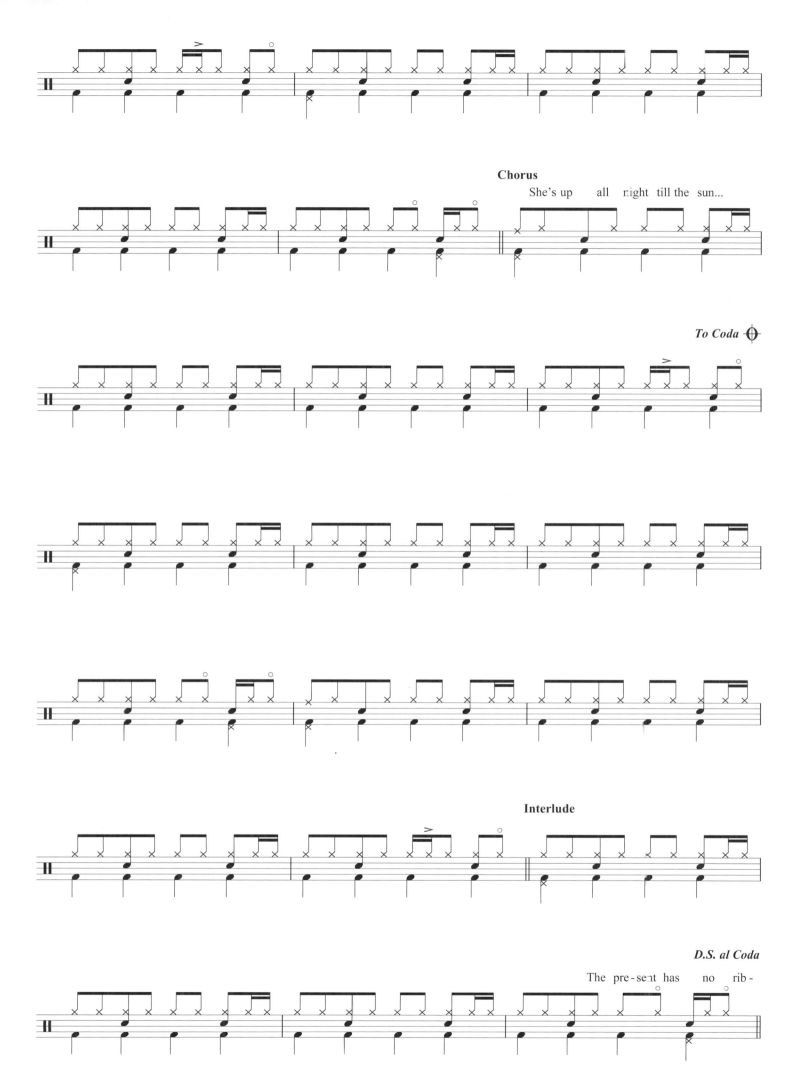

Chorus

She's up   all   night till the sun...

To Coda ⊕

Interlude

D.S. al Coda

The pre-sent has   no   rib-

Coda

We're up all night till the sun...

Play 6 times

Bridge

Pre-Chorus

We've   come too far...

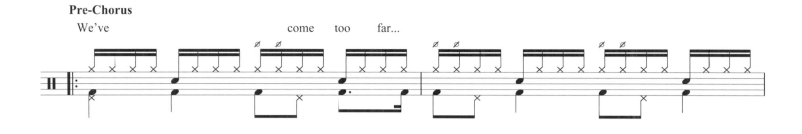

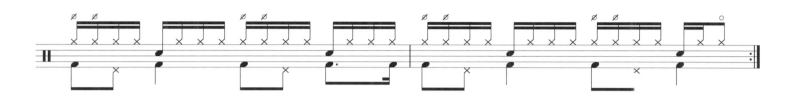

Chorus

She's up   all   night till the   sun...

1., 2., 3.

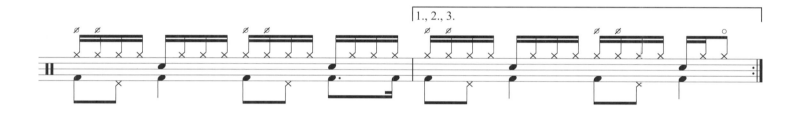

4.

Outro

Begin fade   *Fade out*

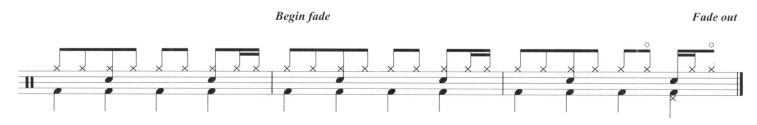

I'm Not the Only One

Words and Music by Sam Smith and James Napier

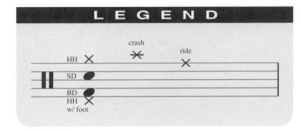

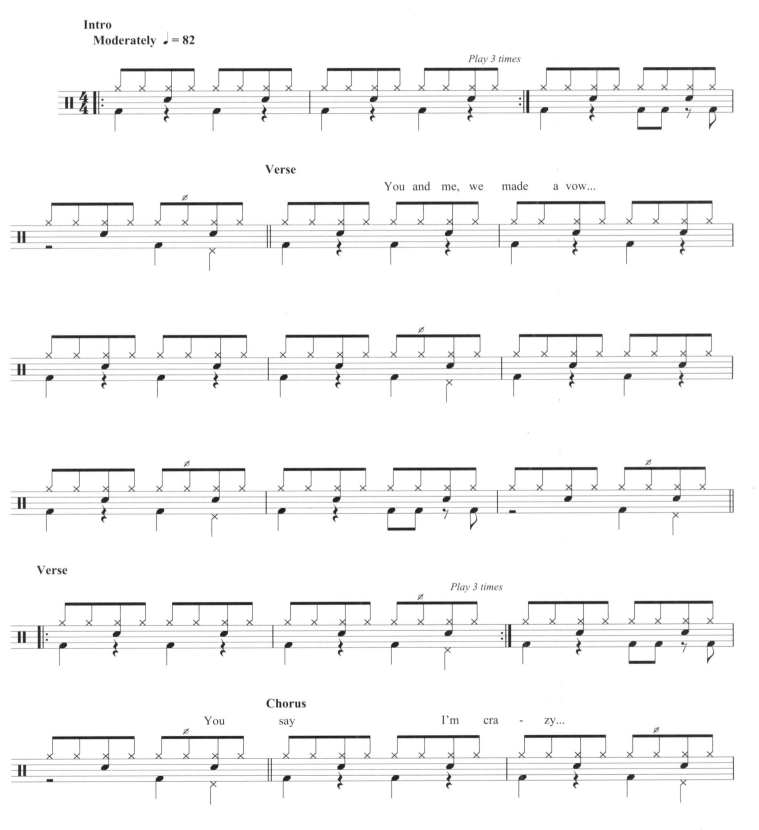

Verse

You've been so un-a-vail-a-ble...

Chorus

You say I'm cra-

- zy...

Play 3 times

Bridge

I have loved you for man-y years...

Chorus

You   say   I'm cra-

- zy...

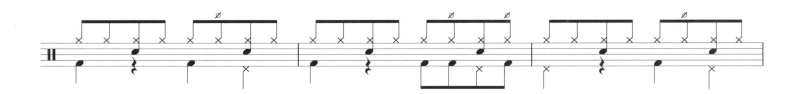

Off the Ground

Words and Music by Marc Cazorla,
Alexander Stiff and Christopher Vos

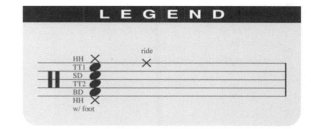

Chorus

Interlude

And   I   got-ta

hunt my - self down   a brand - new home.

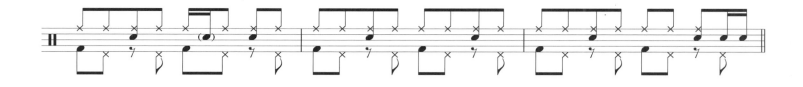

Bridge

Guitar Solo

Verse

I got-ta   get my-self up...

Chorus

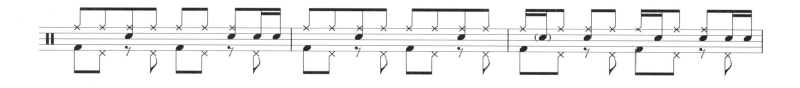

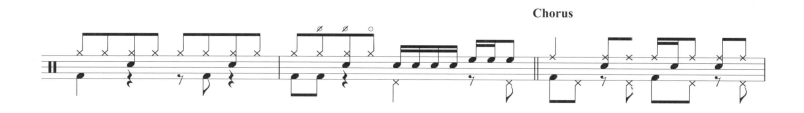

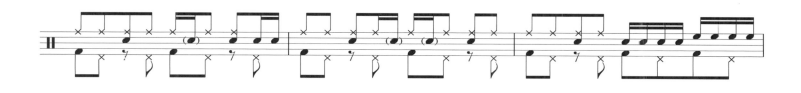

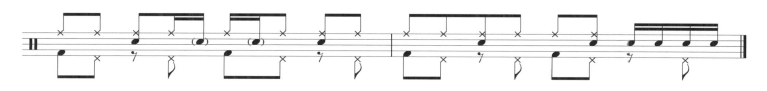

Lonely Boy

Words and Music by Dan Auerbach, Patrick Carney and Brian Burton

Chorus

Play 4 times

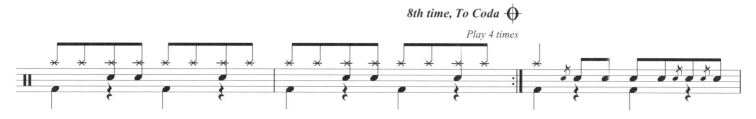

8th time, To Coda ⊕

Play 4 times

3rd time, D.S. al Coda
(take repeats)

Well,   your

Play 3 times

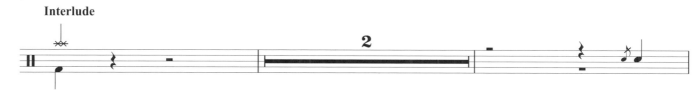

⊕ **Coda**

Interlude

2

Play 4 times

Chorus

Play 3 times

Mercy

Words and Music by Shawn Mendes,
Teddy Geiger, Danny Parker and Ilsey Juber

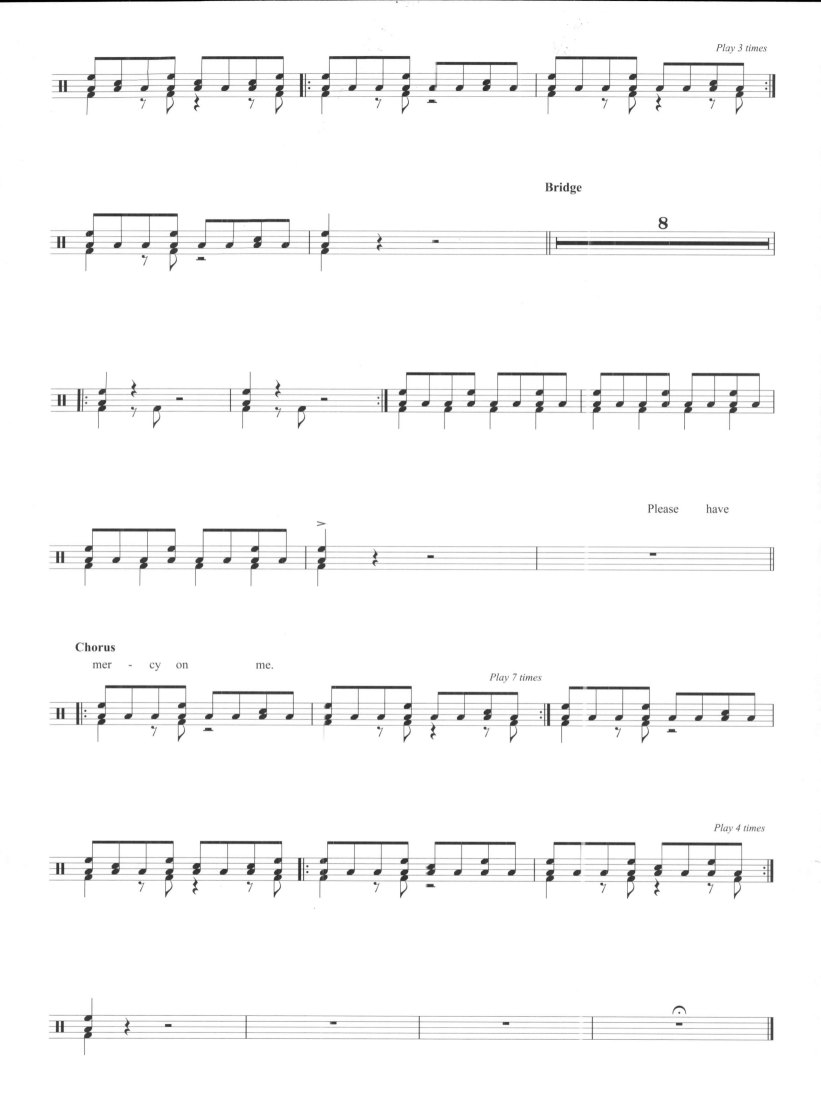

Bridge

8

Please   have

Chorus

mer - cy   on   me.

Play 7 times

Play 4 times

Moves Like Jagger

Words and Music by Adam Levine, Benjamin Levin,
Ammar Malik and Johan Schuster

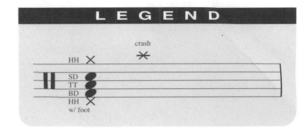

Chorus

Take me by the tongue,

and I'll know you.

Verse

You wan - na know...

Chorus

Take me by the tongue, and I'll know you.

Outro

Ophelia

Words and Music by Jeremy Fraites and Wesley Schultz

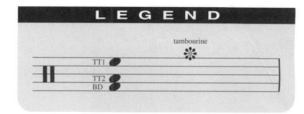

Interlude

Bridge

I, I   got a lit - tle pay -   check...

Chorus

Oh, O - phe - li - a...

Play 4 times   *Play 3 times*

Paradise

Words and Music by Guy Berryman, Jon Buckland,
Will Champion, Chris Martin and Brian Eno

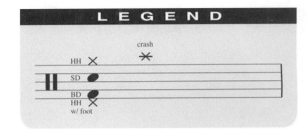

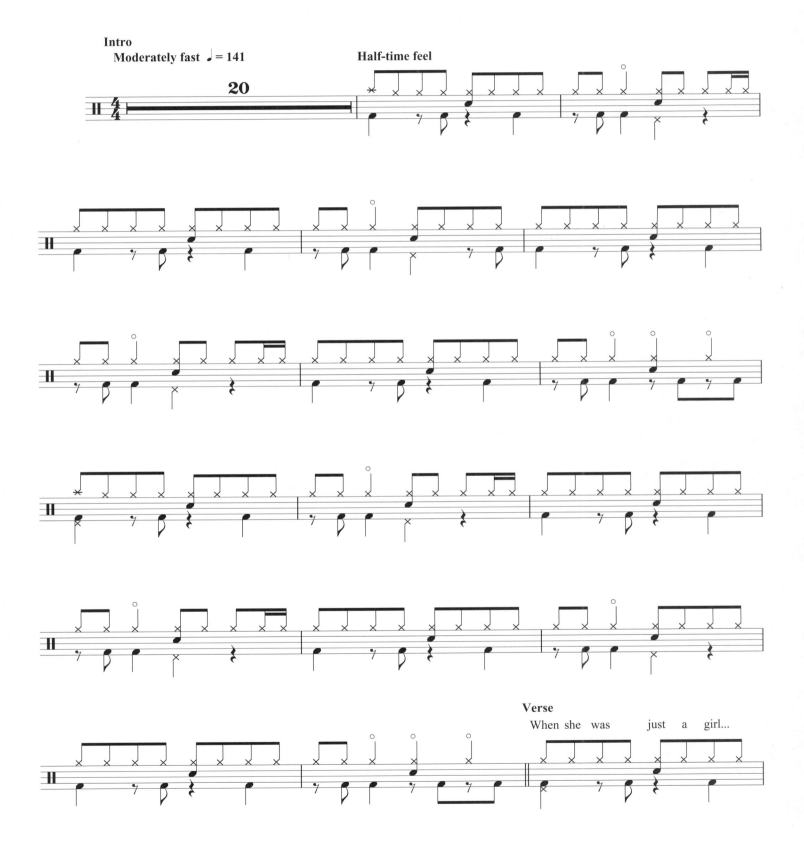

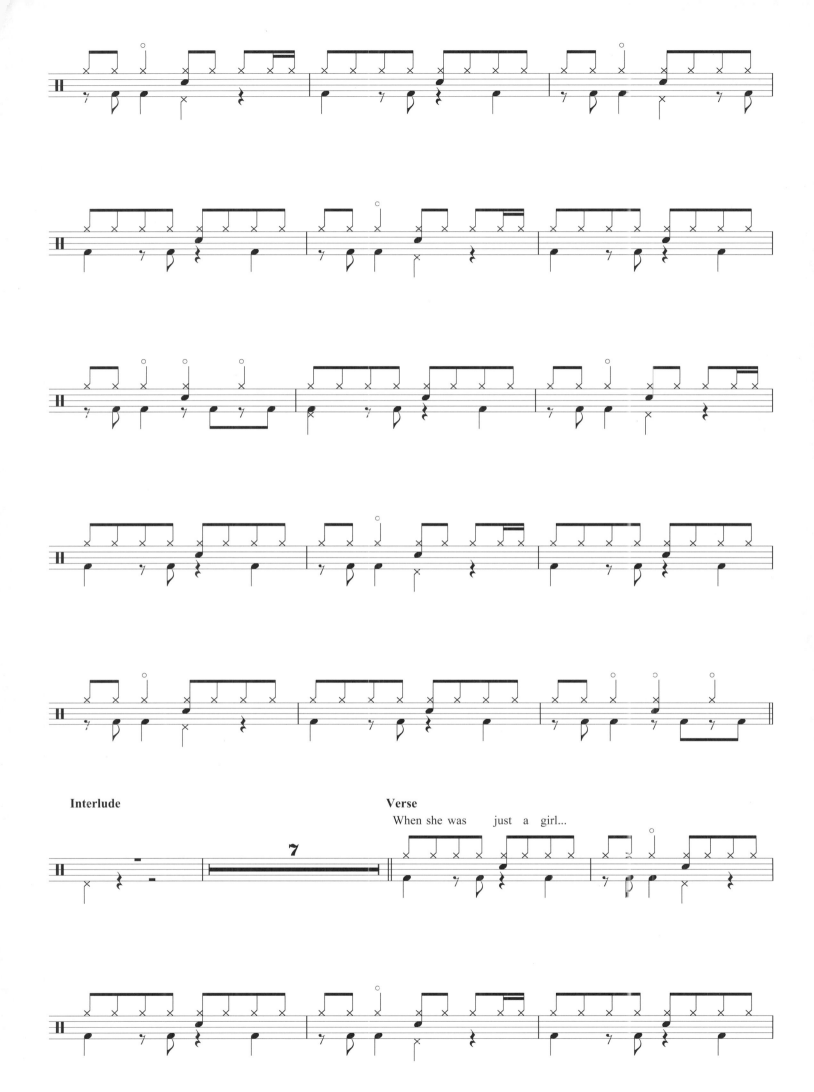

Interlude

7

Verse

When she was   just a girl...

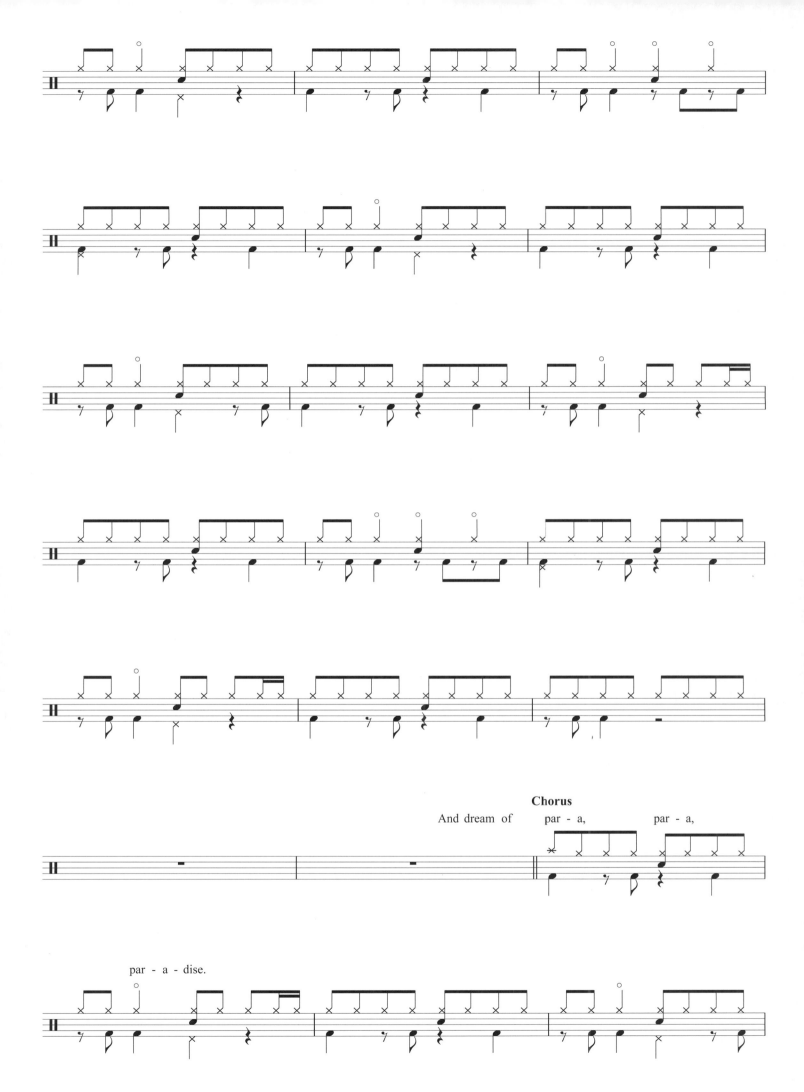

Chorus

And dream of   par - a,   par - a,

par - a - dise.

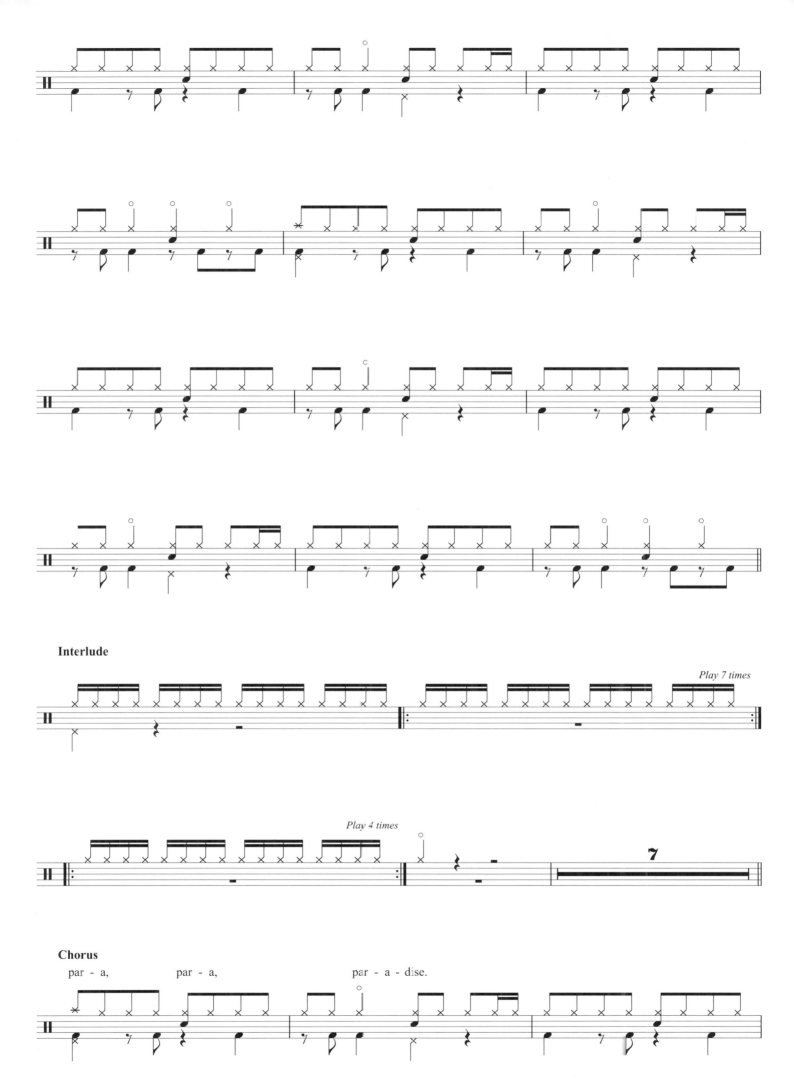

Interlude

Play 7 times

Play 4 times

7

Chorus

par - a,   par - a,   par - a - dise.

Outro

Rolling in the Deep

Words and Music by Adele Adkins and Paul Epworth

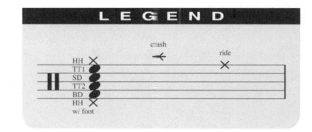

Verse

Ba - by, I have no sto - ry to be told...

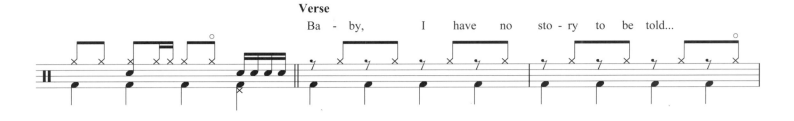

Pre-Chorus

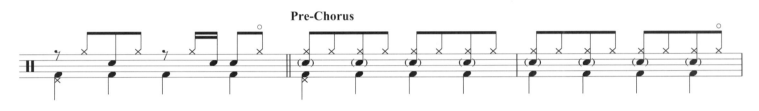

D.S. al Coda

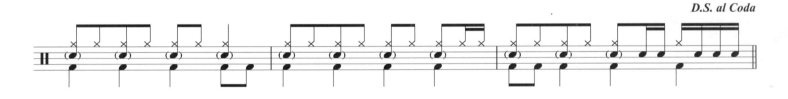

Coda

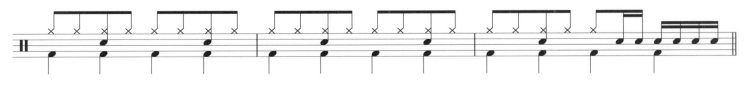

Verse

Throw your   soul   through   ev-er-y   o - pen door...

Radioactive

Words and Music by Daniel Reynolds, Benjamin McKee,
Daniel Sermon, Alexander Grant and Josh Mosser

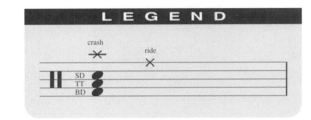

To Coda

Verse

I raise my flag...

D.S. al Coda

Coda

Bridge

Pre-Chorus

I feel it in my bones...

Chorus

I'm

ra - di - o - ac - tive...

Roar

Words and Music by Katy Perry, Max Martin,
Dr. Luke, Bonnie McKee and Henry Walter

Intro
Moderately slow ♩ = 90

Verse

I used to bite my tongue and hold _ my breath...

Play 4 times

Pre-Chorus

Play 4 times

Chorus

Play 7 times

Verse

Now I'm float - in' like   a   but - ter - fly...

Pre-Chorus

Play 4 times

Chorus

Play 7 times

Play 7 times

Interlude

pp

f

Chorus

Play 7 times

Play 7 times

Shake It Off

Words and Music by Taylor Swift, Max Martin and Shellback

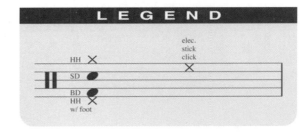

Pre-Chorus

Play 3 times

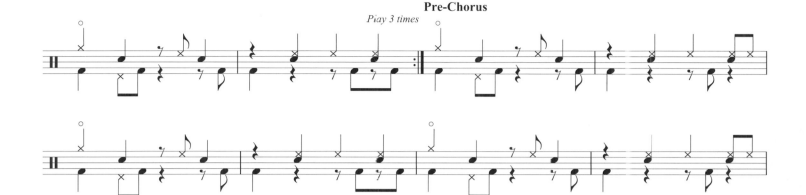

Chorus

Bridge

Play 3 times

1. 2.

Chorus

2

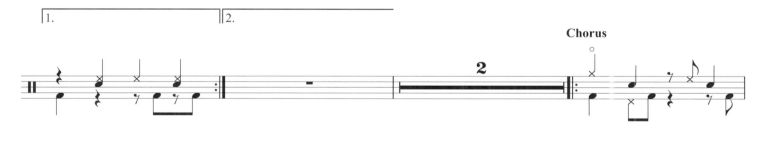

Play 4 times

Shut Up and Dance

Words and Music by Ryan McMahon, Ben Berger,
Sean Waugaman, Eli Maiman, Nicholas Petricca and Kevin Ray

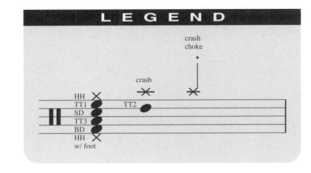

Pre-Chorus

She took my arm...

§ **Chorus**

"Oh, don't you   dare   look back,   just keep your   eyes   on   me."

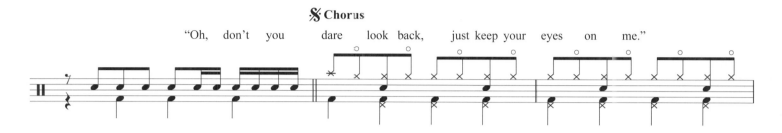

To Coda ⊕

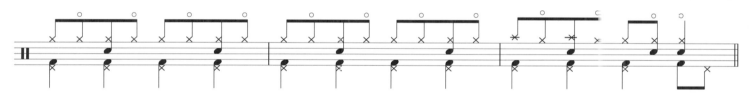

Interlude   **Verse**

A back - less   dress   and some beat - up   sneaks...

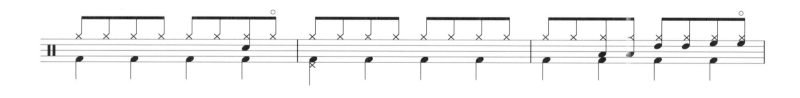

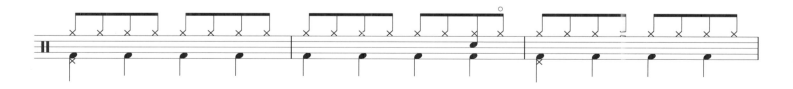

Pre-Chorus

She took my arm...

D.S. al Coda

Coda

Synth Solo

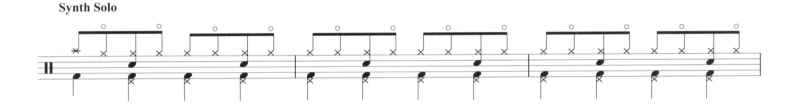

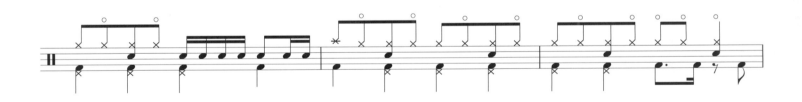

Pre-Chorus

Deep in her eyes...

Interlude

Play 3 times

"Oh, don't you

Chorus

dare look   back,   just keep your   eyes   on   me."

Play 3 times

Chorus

1.

2.

3.

Stressed Out

Words and Music by Tyler Joseph

LEGEND

Intro
Moderately slow ♩ = 85

Verse

I wish I found some bet-ter sounds...

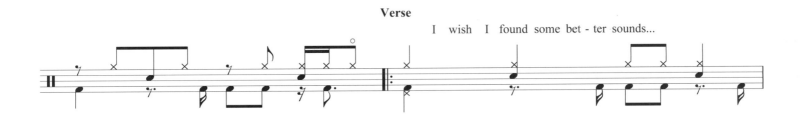

Pre-Chorus

Play 3 times

Chorus

Wish we could turn back time...

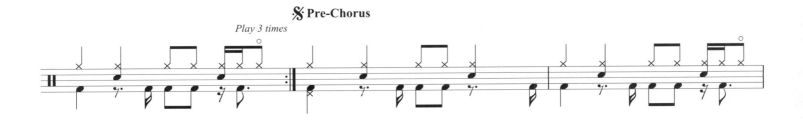

Verse

Some-times, a   cer - tain smell...

D.S. al Coda

⊕ **Coda**

Bridge

We   used   to   play   pre - tend...

Chorus

Outro
We used to play pre-tend...

Take Me to Church

Words and Music by Andrew Hozier-Byrne

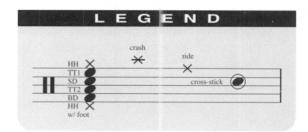

Take me to church...

Verse

If I'm a pa - gan of the good   times...

Take me   to church...

Chorus

Bridge

No mas - ters   or kings...

Pre-Chorus

A -   men.   Take me to church...

Chorus

Thinking Out Loud

Words and Music by Ed Sheeran and Amy Wadge

Verse
Moderately slow ♩ = 79

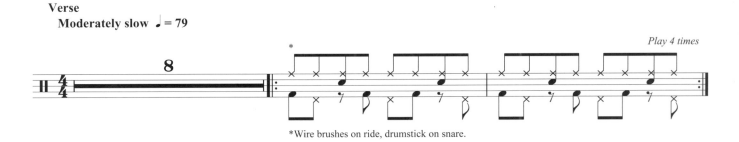

*Wire brushes on ride, drumstick on snare.

Pre-Chorus

peo - ple fall in love in mys - ter - i - ous ways...

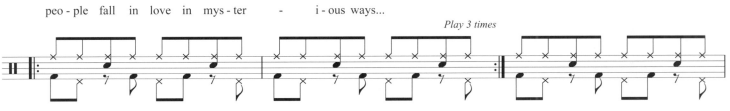

Chorus

So, hon - ey, now...

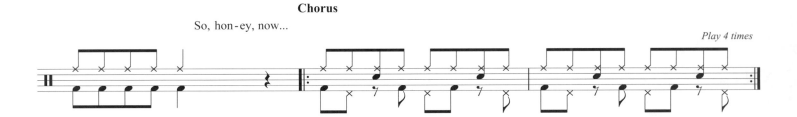

Verse

Pre-Chorus

peo - ple fall in love in mys - ter - i - ous ways...

Chorus

That hon-ey, now...

Play 4 times

Guitar Solo

Play 3 times

Outro-Chorus

So, ba - by, now...

Play 4 times

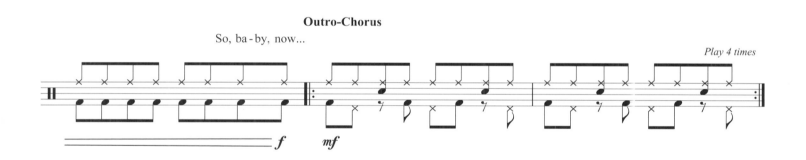

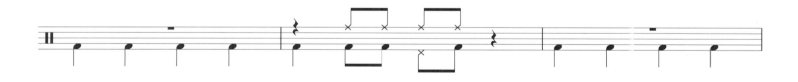

24K Magic

Words and Music by Bruno Mars, Philip Lawrence and Chris Brown

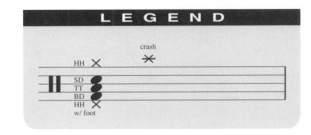

Verse

Sec-ond verse for the hust-lers...

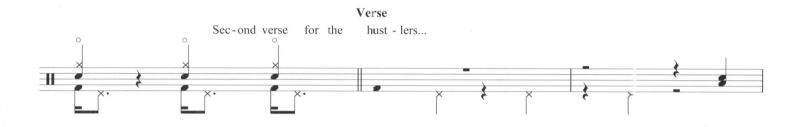

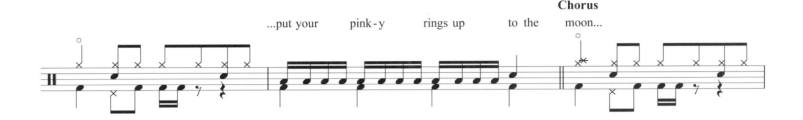

...put your   pink - y   rings up   to the   **Chorus**
moon...

Verse

Ev-'ry-where I   go,   they be like...

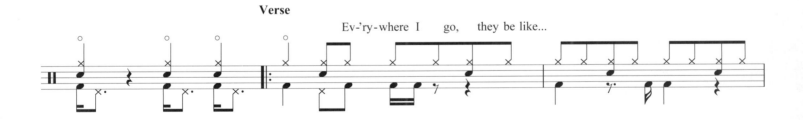

1.   2.

Bridge

Twen-ty-four kar-at...

...put your   pink-y   rings up   to the   moon...   **Chorus**

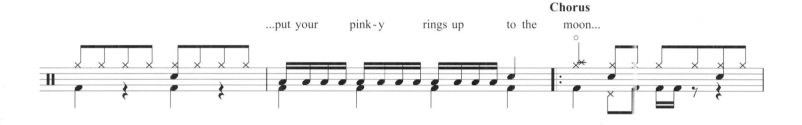

1.

2.

Unsteady

Words and Music by Alexander Junior Grant, Adam Levin,
Casey Harris, Noah Feldshuh and Sam Harris

𝄋 Chorus

Hold,   hold   on...

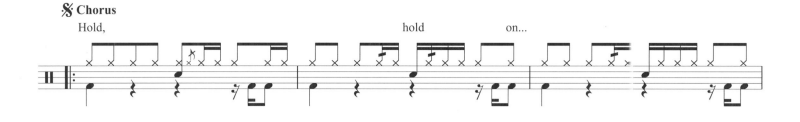

1., 2.   3.   4.

To Coda ⊕

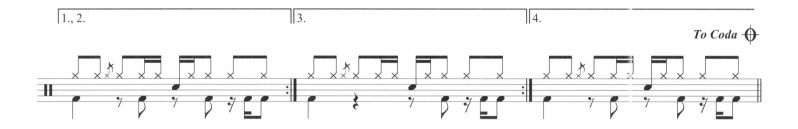

Verse

Moth - er,   I   know...

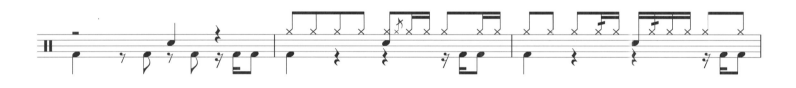

Pre-Chorus

But if   you   love

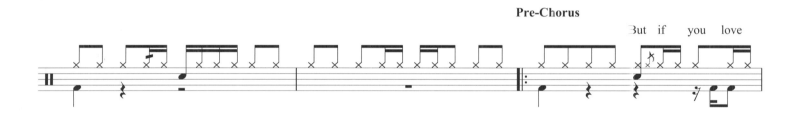

1.

me,   don't let   go.

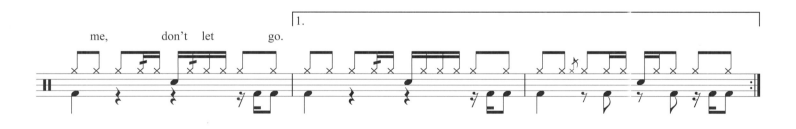

2.

D.S. al Coda
(take repeats)

⊕ **Coda**
Outro

8

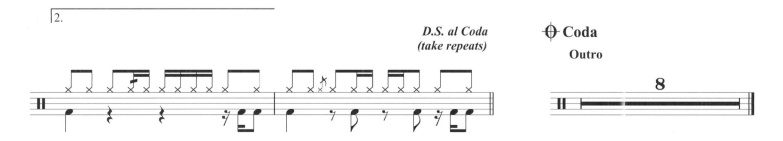

Uptown Funk

Words and Music by Mark Ronson, Bruno Mars, Philip Lawrence,
Jeff Bhasker, Devon Gallaspy, Nicholaus Williams, Lonnie Simmons,
Ronnie Wilson, Charles Wilson, Rudolph Taylor and Robert Wilson

Play 3 times

Verse
Stop!   Wait a min-ute.

Pre-Chorus
Play 3 times

Chorus
Girls   hit   you, hal-le-lu-jah...
Play 4 times   *Play 3 times*

Interlude
Play 3 times

Bridge
Play 3 times

Spoken: 'Fore we leave...

Play 3 times

Interlude

Play 3 times

Outro

Up - town   funk   you   up,   up - town   funk   you   up...

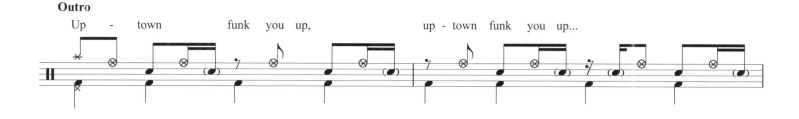

The Walker

Words and Music by Michael Fitzpatrick, Jeremy Ruzumna,
Noelle Scaggs, Joseph Karnes, James Midhi King
and John Meredith Wicks

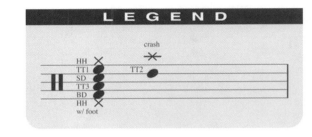

Intro
Moderately fast ♩ = 131

Verse
Ooh, cra - zy's what they think...

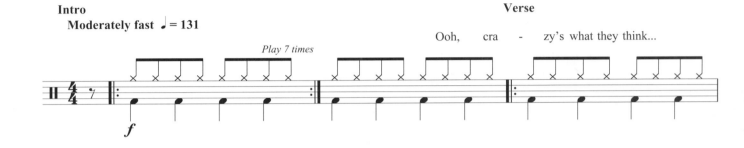

Pre-Chorus

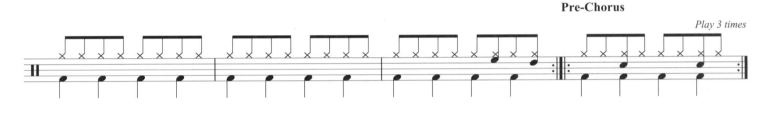

Chorus
Oh,   here we go,   feel it in my soul...

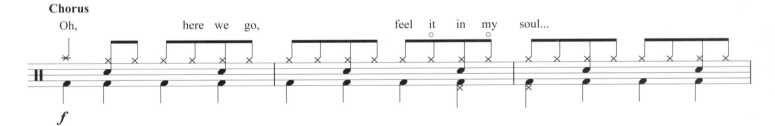

Interlude

Interlude

Interlude

Chorus

Oh,   here we go,   feel it in my

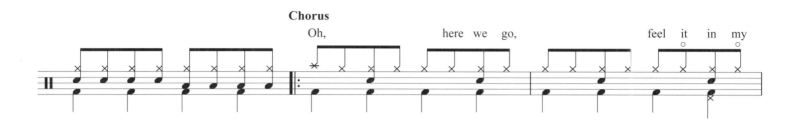

soul...

1.

2.

Outro

Play 7 times

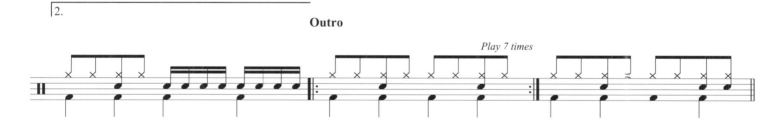

Begin fade

Play 3 times   Play 3 times

Fade out

We Are Young

Words and Music by Jeff Bhasker, Andrew Dost,
Jack Antonoff and Nate Ruess

*Accents apply to toms only throughout.

Verse

know that   I'm not...

Play 3 times

Chorus

To - night,   we   are

1., 2., 3. |4.

young...

Bridge

Car - ry   me   home   to - night...

Play 7 times

Chorus

we   are   young...

1., 2., 3. |4.

Outro

3